Francis Frith's
Leeds

Photographic Memories

Francis Frith's
Leeds

Revised edition of original work by

Clive Hardy

First published in hardback in the United Kingdom in 1998
by WBC Ltd
ISBN 1-85937-272-4

Revised paperback edition published in the United Kingdom in 2000 by
The Francis Frith Collection
ISBN 1-85937-202-3

Reprinted in paperback 2006

British Library Cataloguing in Publication Data

Leeds Photographic Memories
Clive Hardy
ISBN 1-85937-202-3

The Francis Frith Collection
Frith's Barn, Teffont,
Salisbury, Wiltshire SP3 5QP
Tel: +44 (0) 1722 716 376
Email: info@francisfrith.co.uk
www.francisfrith.com

Printed and bound in Great Britain

Front Cover: **LEEDS,** *The Post Office and Revenue Office 1897* 39088t
The colour-tinting in this image is for illustrative purposes only,
and is not intended to be historically accurate

Aerial photographs reproduced under licence from Simmons Aerofilms Limited
Historical Ordnance Survey maps reproduced under licence from Homecheck.co.uk

Every attempt has been made to contact copyright holders of illustrative material.
We will be happy to give full acknowledgement in future editions for any items not credited.
Any information should be directed to The Francis Frith Collection.

AS WITH ANY HISTORICAL DATABASE THE FRITH ARCHIVE IS CONSTANTLY BEING CORRECTED AND IMPROVED
AND THE PUBLISHERS WOULD WELCOME INFORMATION ON OMISSIONS OR INACCURACIES

Contents

Francis Frith: *Victorian Pioneer*

FRANCIS FRITH, Victorian founder of the world-famous photographic archive, was a complex and multitudinous man. A devout Quaker and a highly successful Victorian businessman, he was both philosophic by nature and pioneering in outlook.

By 1855 Francis Frith had already established a wholesale grocery business in Liverpool, and sold it for the astonishing sum of £200,000, which is the equivalent today of over £15,000,000. Now a very rich man, he was able to indulge his passion for travel. As a child he had pored over travel books written by early explorers, and his fancy and imagination had been stirred by family holidays to the sublime mountain regions of Wales and Scotland. 'What a land of spirit-stirring and enriching scenes and places!' he had written. He was to return to these scenes of grandeur in later years to 'recapture the thousands of vivid and tender memories', but with a different purpose. Now in his thirties, and captivated by the new science of photography, Frith set out on a series of pioneering journeys to the Nile regions that occupied him from 1856 until 1860.

Intrigue and Adventure

He took with him on his travels a specially-designed wicker carriage that acted as both dark-room and sleeping chamber. These far-flung journeys were packed with intrigue and adventure. In his life story, written when he was sixty-three, Frith tells of being held captive by bandits, and of fighting 'an awful midnight battle to the very point of surrender with a deadly pack of hungry, wild dogs'. Sporting flowing Arab costume, Frith arrived at Akaba by camel sixty years before Lawrence, where he encountered 'desert princes and rival sheikhs, blazing with jewel-hilted swords'.

During these extraordinary adventures he was assiduously exploring the desert regions bordering the Nile and patiently recording the antiquities and peoples with his camera. He was the first photographer to venture beyond the sixth cataract. Africa was still the mysterious 'Dark Continent', and Stanley and Livingstone's historic meeting was a decade into the future. The conditions for picture taking confound belief. He laboured for hours in his wicker dark-room in the sweltering heat of the desert, while the volatile chemicals fizzed dangerously in their trays. Often he was forced to work in remote tombs and caves where conditions were cooler. Back in London he exhibited his photographs and was 'rapturously cheered' by members of the Royal Society. His reputation as a photographer was made overnight. An eminent modern historian has likened their impact on the population of the time to that on our own generation of the first photographs taken on the surface of the moon.

Venture of a Life-Time

Characteristically, Frith quickly spotted the opportunity to create a new business as a specialist publisher of photographs. He lived in an era of immense and sometimes violent change. For the poor in the early part of Victoria's reign work was a drudge and the hours long, and people had precious little free time to enjoy themselves. Most had no transport other than a cart or gig at their disposal, and had not travelled far beyond the boundaries of their own town or village. However, by the 1870s, the railways had threaded their way across the country, and Bank Holidays and half-day Saturdays had been made obligatory by Act of Parliament. All of a sudden the ordinary working man and his family were able to enjoy days out and see a little more of the world.

With characteristic business acumen, Francis Frith foresaw that these new tourists would enjoy having souvenirs to commemorate their days out. In 1860 he married Mary Ann Rosling and set out with the intention of photographing every city, town and village in Britain. For the next thirty years he travelled the country by train and by pony and trap, producing fine photographs of seaside resorts and beauty spots that were keenly bought by millions of Victorians. These prints were painstakingly pasted into family albums and pored over during the dark nights of winter, rekindling precious memories of summer excursions.

The Rise of Frith & Co

Frith's studio was soon supplying retail shops all over the country. To meet the demand he gathered about him a small team of photographers, and published the work of independent artist-photographers of the calibre of Roger Fenton and Francis Bedford. In order to gain some understanding of the scale of Frith's business one only has to look at the catalogue issued by Frith & Co in 1886: it runs to some 670 pages, listing not only many thousands of views of the British Isles but also many photographs of most European countries, and China, Japan, the USA and

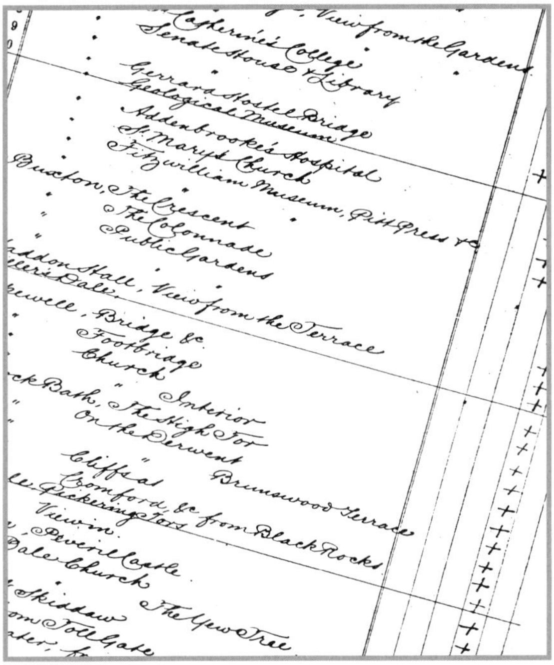
Catherine's College, View from the Gardens
Senate House & Library
Gerrard Hostel Bridge
Geological Museum
Addenbrooke's Hospital
St Mary's Church
Fitzwilliam Museum, Pitt Press &c
Buxton, The Crescent
The Colonnade
Public Gardens
ddon Hall, View from the Terrace
llers Dale
ewell, Bridge &c.
Footbridge
Church
ck Bath, " Interior
The High Tor
On the Derwent
Cliffs at " Brunswood Terrace
Cromford, &c from Black Rocks
le Pickering Tors
View in
Peveril Castle
Dale Church
Skiddaw The Yew Tree
om Toll Gate

Canada – note the sample page shown above from the hand-written *Frith & Co* ledgers detailing pictures taken. By 1890 Frith had created the greatest specialist photographic publishing company in the world, with over 2,000 outlets – more than the combined number that Boots and WH Smith have today! The picture on the right shows the *Frith & Co* display board at Ingleton in the Yorkshire Dales (left of window). Beautifully constructed with a mahogany frame and gilt inserts, it could display up to a dozen local scenes.

Postcard Bonanza

The ever-popular holiday postcard we know today took many years to develop. In 1870 the Post Office issued the first plain cards, with a pre-printed stamp on one face. In 1894 they allowed other publishers' cards to be sent through the mail with an attached adhesive halfpenny stamp. Demand grew rapidly, and in 1895 a new size of postcard was permitted called the court card, but there was little room for illustration. In 1899, a year after Frith's death, a new card measuring 5.5 x 3.5 inches became the standard format, but it was not until 1902 that the divided back came into being, with address and message on one face and a full-size illustration on the other. *Frith & Co* were in the vanguard of postcard development, and Frith's sons Eustace and Cyril continued their father's monumental task, expanding the number of views offered to the public and recording more and more places in Britain, as the coasts and countryside were opened up to mass travel.

Francis Frith died in 1898 at his villa in Cannes, his great project still growing. The archive he created continued in business for another seventy years. By 1970 it contained over a third of a million pictures of 7,000 cities, towns and villages. The massive photographic record Frith has left to us stands as a living monument to a special and very remarkable man.

Frith's Archive: *A Unique Legacy*

FRANCIS FRITH'S legacy to us today is of immense significance and value, for the magnificent archive of evocative photographs he created provides a unique record of change in 7,000 cities, towns and villages throughout Britain over a century and more. Frith and his fellow studio photographers revisited locations many times down the years to update their views, compiling for us an enthralling and colourful pageant of British life and character.

We tend to think of Frith's sepia views of Britain as nostalgic, for most of us use them to conjure up memories of places in our own lives with which we have family associations. It often makes us forget that to Francis Frith they were records of daily life as it was actually being lived in the cities, towns and villages of his day. The Victorian age was one of great and often bewildering change for ordinary people, and though the pictures evoke an impression of slower times, life was as busy and hectic as it is today.

See Frith at www.francisfrith.com

We are fortunate that Frith was a photographer of the people, dedicated to recording the minutiae of everyday life. For it is this sheer wealth of visual data, the painstaking chronicle of changes in dress, transport, street layouts, buildings, housing, engineering and landscape that captivates us so much today. His remarkable images offer us a powerful link with the past and with the lives of our ancestors.

Today's Technology

Computers have now made it possible for Frith's many thousands of images to be accessed almost instantly. In the Frith archive today, each photograph is carefully 'digitised' then stored on a CD Rom. Frith archivists can locate a single photograph amongst thousands within seconds. Views can be catalogued and sorted under a variety of categories of place and content to the immediate benefit of researchers.

Inexpensive reference prints can be created for them at the touch of a mouse button, and a wide range of books and other printed materials assembled and published for a wider, more general readership - in the next twelve months over a hundred Frith local history titles will be published! The day-to-day workings of the archive are very different from how they were in Francis Frith's time: imagine the herculean task of sorting through eleven tons of glass negatives as Frith had to do to locate a particular sequence of pictures! Yet the archive still prides itself on maintaining the same high standards of excellence laid down by Francis Frith, including the painstaking cataloguing and indexing of every view.

It is curious to reflect on how the internet now allows researchers in America and elsewhere greater instant access to the archive than Frith himself ever enjoyed. Many thousands of individual views can be called up on screen within seconds on one of the Frith internet sites, enabling people living continents away to revisit the streets of their ancestral home town, or view places in Britain where they have enjoyed holidays. Many overseas researchers welcome the chance to view special theme selections, such as transport, sports, costume and ancient monuments.

We are certain that Francis Frith would have heartily approved of these modern developments in imaging techniques, for he himself was always working at the very limits of Victorian photographic technology.

The Value of the Archive Today

Because of the benefits brought by the computer, Frith's images are increasingly studied by social historians, by researchers into genealogy and ancestory, by architects, town planners, and by teachers and schoolchildren involved in local history projects.

In addition, the archive offers every one of us an opportunity to examine the places where we and our families have lived and worked down the years. Highly successful in Frith's own era, the archive is now, a century and more on, entering a new phase of popularity.

The Past in Tune with the Future

Historians consider the Francis Frith Collection to be of prime national importance. It is the only archive of its kind remaining in private ownership and has been valued at a million pounds. However, this figure is now rapidly increasing as digital technology enables more and more people around the world to enjoy its benefits.

Francis Frith's archive is now housed in an historic timber barn in the beautiful village of Teffont in Wiltshire. Its founder would not recognize the archive office as it is today. In place of the many thousands of dusty boxes containing glass plate negatives and an all-pervading odour of photographic chemicals, there are now ranks of computer screens. He would be amazed to watch his images travelling round the world at unimaginable speeds through network and internet lines.

The archive's future is both bright and exciting. Francis Frith, with his unshakeable belief in making photographs available to the greatest number of people, would undoubtedly approve of what is being done today with his lifetime's work. His photographs, depicting our shared past, are now bringing pleasure and enlightenment to millions around the world a century and more after his death.

Leeds - *An Introduction*

Leeds was the industrial powerhouse of the West Riding, and like all our great industrial cities, it grew from much humbler beginnings. When the Domesday Book was being compiled, Leeds was little more than an agricultural village huddled between the river and what is now Kirkgate. There were 35 families, a priest, a church and a mill - the latter doing well enough to be worth four shillings a year.

The village was under the lordship of Ilbert de Lacy, William the Conqueror's deputy in those parts, and as such appears to have escaped the wrath of the Conqueror when he laid waste to much of Yorkshire following an uprising in 1070. Around 1100 de Lacy sublet Leeds to Ralph Paganel, who was also the tenant-in-chief of Headingley and other lands throughout the county. Paganel, rich and powerful in his own right, was appointed High Sheriff of Yorkshire in 1110.

In Leeds and the surrounding villages, cloth manufacture seems to have been underway on a small scale by the 12th century, almost certainly influenced by the close proximity of the Cistercian abbey of Kirkstall. Endowed by Henry de Lacy in thanks to the Blessed Virgin Kirkstall, like the Cistercian abbeys of Fountains, Rievaulx and Jervaulx, kept huge flocks of sheep for wool. In the 12th century most of the wool was sold for weaving in Flanders and Northern Italy, though there was a considerable amount of weaving done at both York and later Beverley, with Leeds, Wakefield, Whitby and Selby the poor relations. By the late 14th century, however, times were changing. The guilds at York and Beverley were so over-regulated and over-taxed with guild levies that they were unable to rise to the challenge of cheaper textiles from the likes of Leeds, Halifax and Wakefield, where production costs were lower. Even so, as late as 1470 Leeds was still being described as 'near Rothwell'. Yet within the next 50 years the town would emerge as the leading centre in Yorkshire for the trade in woollen cloths, and by 1560 was probably similar in size to Bradford. There were houses on both sides of Briggate as far as the Headrow, and others beyond Timble Bridge over Sheepscar Beck. The population at this time would have been around 3,000, if the outlying hamlets of Woodhouse, Buslingthorpe, Potternewton and Knowsthorpe are taken into consideration.

By 1612 the population had probably doubled, due in part to people coming to the town in search of work. Building development now extended along Kirkgate, Boar Lane, Vicar Lane and Swinegate: an ever-growing mixture of housing and workshops sprung up, as Leeds' position within the textile industry continued to strengthen. The town was no longer simply engaged in manufacturing: it had become the leading finishing centre in the West Riding for cropping, dyeing and dressing. Leeds merchants traded aggressively both at home and abroad, securing markets previously dominated by the merchants of York, Beverley and Hull.

Leeds and the Civil War

In January 1643, Sir William Savile entered Leeds at the head of a Royalist force of 500 horsemen and 1,500 foot soldiers. He set about fortifying the town: artillery was sited to cover Briggate, earthworks were thrown up at the north end of Leeds Bridge and a trench was dug around the town perimeter to the banks of the Aire. On 23rd January Sir Thomas Fairfax, at the head of a Parliamentarian force of 3,000 men, crossed the Aire at Apperley Bridge and halted on Woodhouse Moor. Sir Thomas followed the rules of engagement of the day by offering Sir William terms. Sir William declined and the assault began at around 2pm. Within two hours the Parliamentarians had broken through the defences and the battle was soon over. Though Sir William escaped, 500 of his men were taken prisoner but, as was the custom, they were allowed to go free after promising to take no further part in the war.

In 1646 Charles I was held prisoner for one night at the Red Hall in Upper Head Row. One of the stories surrounding the king's short stay in Leeds concerns John Harrison, a wealthy landowner. On hearing that the king was being held in Leeds, Harrison asked permission to meet with him and present him with a tankard of ale. The king accepted Harrison's offer and on opening the lid of the tankard found it full of golden guineas which 'his Majesty did, with

Boar Lane c1965
extract from L28148

much celerity, hasten to secrete about his royal person'.

Powerhouse of West Riding

By 1600 Leeds had established itself as the most important of all the cloth fairs in the county. Every Tuesday and Saturday tables were set up on the bridge over the Aire at the bottom of Briggate. When the market bell tolled the sellers would move to the tables, which they had to share, and stand in line behind their pieces. The traders entered when the bell stopped tolling. Business was done in a whisper so that other buyers and sellers could not overhear the price agreed. After a couple of hours the bell tolled to signal the end of the market and everything was cleared away. Daniel Defoe reckoned that in a morning somewhere between £10,000-£20,000 worth of cloth was traded.

By 1710 these open-air markets were being challenged by Cloth Halls, where business could be done whatever the weather outside. Leeds answered the challenge in 1711 with the opening of a hall for White Cloths. In 1755 a new and much larger purpose-built White Cloth Hall was opened, followed a few months later by a Mixed Cloth Hall.

By 1775 the population of Leeds is thought to have been about 17,000 and by the time of the first census of 1801 it had rocketed to 53,000. The coming of the factory system led to thousands leaving the countryside in search of work. The work they found was alien to them: strict discipline, regular attendance, long hours and unsafe working practices. Yorkshire mill owners were at the forefront when it came to employing child labour in almost slave-like conditions. Many of these children were sent north from London workhouses. Those who ended up in the mills around Leeds were luckier than the children sent to Bradford. In Leeds they worked a 12-hour day; in Bradford, 13. In both places children were beaten to keep them awake.

With the factory system came machinery. As with every subsequent generation, the factory workers of the early 19th century equated mechanisation with a threat to jobs. In the 1800s reaction to the threat manifested itself in the movement that came to be known as Luddism. The earliest cases in Yorkshire date from 1811 to 1812 when croppers rebelled against the introduction of shearing frames.

West Yorkshire's most famous Luddite was George Mellor. On 6th January 1813, George Mellor, William Thorpe and Thomas Smith were indicted before the grand jury at York Castle with the wilful murder of William Horsfall, merchant and manufacturer. With a former accomplice Benjamin Walker turning king's evidence, they had little chance and were executed at York. A few days later seven men went on trial charged with attacking William Cartwright's mill. Cartwright had already taken the precaution of arranging for troops to help guard his premises. When the Luddites attacked the troops opened fire. In an attack lasting about 20 minutes, both sides exchanged fire and several men died of their wounds. Found guilty, the Luddites were sentenced to death and executed at York.

It was the combination of the factory system and the application of steam power that led to the concentration of textile production in a handful of towns, including Bradford, Huddersfield, Dewsbury, Batley, Bingley and Leeds. By the mid-19th century there was an enormous diversity in the manufacturing base of the town. Though woollens still dominated the scene, the flax industry employed over 9,000 workers and other industries included rope, glass, earthenware and paper manufacturing.

Coalmining was a major industry in the area. At its height there were 102 collieries employing 5,000 miners, with an annual total output of 2.5 million tons. Engineering also played an important part in the development of Leeds. Fairbairn & Lawson manufactured flax and tow machinery, much of which went for export.

The area also became a centre for the manufacture of railway locomotives, with such firms as Todd, Kitson & Laird, Fenton, Murray & Jackson, and E B Wilson & Co. When E B Wilson & Co closed in the 1850s much of the equipment and patterns were purchased by Manning, Wardle & Co, with the result that Manning's early locomotives looked like E B Wilson's products.

In 1860 yet another locomotive manufacturer appeared on the scene with the opening of Hudswell, Clarke & Co, followed in 1864 by the Hunslet Engine Co. The latter would be the last of the Leeds locomotive builders to remain in business, surviving into the 1990s. By the 1850s, Kitson's Airedale foundry was turning out traction, stationary and ploughing engines for John Fowler, though Fowler eventually opened his own works.

Later still, Samuel Fox developed pressed-steel railway bogies and wagon underframes. Though Leeds had become a major engineering centre, iron-making was always on a small scale and even in 1871 there were only two blast furnaces in the borough. There were, however, a large number of foundries, such as the Leeds Forge Co and Kirkstall Forge Co, producing all manner of castings. Towards the end of the 19th century the production of wrought iron declined as steel gained in popularity. Most firms switched to using steel imported from Middlesborough, Sheffield and Rotherham.

In the 1870s, Leeds was smoke-covered and overcrowded. Three-quarters of the population was crammed into one-eighth of the area of the borough, in some of the most appalling housing in existence. As more and more people had flocked to Leeds in search of work, cheap housing had been thrown up to accommodate them, often without any thought being given to sewage disposal or water supply. The result was that infectious diseases were often rife in working-class areas: cholera epidemics killed 700 in 1832 and over 2,000 in 1848-49. One tourist attraction in Wellington Yard in 1872 was a midden 6 ft deep, 6 ft wide and 21 ft long.

There had been little or no regulation regarding the building of workers' housing. For example,

Briggate c1955
extract from L28012

Johnson's Square comprised 15 single-room houses situated below the level of Charles Street; Camp Field off Water Lane comprised 92 back-to-back houses built in an area of just 70 yds by 125 yds. Another feature of local housing was the blind-backs, which had no rear windows or doors. From the end elevation they looked like a house that had been cut in half with one half pulled down. Some blind-backs were built up against factory walls, and others were built so that they looked like ordinary houses from the outside with a central porch. In fact, these were two blind-backs, each consisting of four single-room houses, probably accommodating 30 or more people.

It has been estimated that by 1881 around 80 per cent of England's population was living in towns, compared with only 25 per cent in 1800. Though Leeds continued to play a major role in the woollen industry, competition was increasing and several large mills diversified into dyeing and finishing. By the 1891 census the textile industry was employing 22,313 workers, a slight reduction over 1881; but clothing manufacturing had nearly doubled to 30,172 employees. Over the period 1881-1891, an additional 23,000 manufacturing and 32,000 transport, professional and service-sector jobs had been created in Leeds, and the total population had risen from 309,835 to 366,129. Still Leeds continued to grow. By 1901 the population stood at 428,744 and by 1911 it was 445,791. It was all far removed from the tiny hamlet of 1085.

By Road

Leeds' rise into becoming one of the leading industrial centres in the country was also due in part to the development of transport and communication links - not only throughout West Yorkshire but with Lancashire, the Midlands, the north-east and London. By the mid 18th century what passed for the existing road network was under severe strain, unable to cope with increasing and often heavy freight traffic generated by the expanding woollen industry, collieries and agriculture. The two principal turnpikes in the area were the Leeds to Ripon via Harrogate, and the Leeds to Skipton. Turnpikes offered a system of reasonably well-maintained roads for the first time since the Roman occupation. In the 1750s the journey from Leeds to London took at least four days. By the end of the 18th century, turnpikes helped make the journey possible in just over one day. They enabled scheduled daily stagecoach services to operate, strengthening the town's links with York, Hull, Sheffield, Manchester, Birmingham, Carlisle and London. The Leeds-to-Bradford turnpike was one of the busiest, carrying large quantities of freight as well as passenger traffic. In 1778 tolls on this road amounted to £852; by 1798 the sum was £2,843 and in 1810 it had risen to £4,445.

By 1830 Leeds was one of the busiest coaching interchanges in the provinces, with well over 100 daily scheduled services leaving the coaching inns in Briggate. Both long-distance and short-haul freight services were operated to and from Leeds, the town having no fewer than 180 haulage businesses, many of which had their offices in local inns, where business could be conducted over a bottle of brandy or a few jugs of ale.

In 1835 coaching was at its peak with around 3,300 stagecoaches and over 700 mail coaches operating daily scheduled services. However the writing was already on the wall. As early as 1830 the Post Office had contracted the Liverpool & Manchester Railway to carry mail.

By Water

In November 1700, the Aire and Calder was open for navigation as far as Leeds Bridge, where a wharf and a warehouse had been built on the north bank. Cloth could now be loaded for Hull, London, the Baltic and the Low Countries. The obvious advantage that water transport had over the roads was that of cost. It was far cheaper to send 20 tons of coal to Hull by way of the Aire and Calder than it was to hire sufficient wagons to do the same job.

By 1760 river navigation was possible to Elland and Halifax, but the real prize would be the linking of the Humber with the Mersey. In 1770 the Leeds & Liverpool Canal was sanctioned. At 127 miles in length excluding branches, the canal was the longest in Britain. The first section, Bingley to Skipton, was opened by 1773 and in 1777 the sections from Aire and Calder at Leeds to Gargrave, and from Wigan to Liverpool were open for traffic. Then the money ran out. In 1790 a new Act allowed funds to be raised for construction of the middle section, but following the outbreak of war with France the funding slowed down and it was not until 1816 that the canal was open throughout.

One of the problems suffered by the Leeds & Liverpool was lack of adequate water supplies. In long dry summers some sections had to be closed for weeks at a time, and despite the heavy payloads capable of being carried, carriers were forced to seek a reliable alternative.

By Rail

In June 1758 the Middleton Railway became the first in Britain to be sanctioned under an Act of Parliament. Built to a gauge of 4 ft 1 in, the Middleton ran to a coal staith south of Leeds Bridge. The staith was built to supply the town at a guaranteed price of just over 10s a ton. Other collieries in the area were unable to compete and as a result Middleton had a virtual monopoly on the coal sold in Leeds.

The Middleton was worked by horses until 1812 when steam locomotives made an appearance. Steam traction continued until 1835, when horses once again took over. Steam locomotives were reintroduced in 1866 and the line converted to standard gauge in 1881.

Main-line railways came to Leeds in 1834 with the opening of the Leeds & Selby line. The effect upon the Aire and Calder Navigation was almost immediate and the company had little alternative but to slash its freight charges in an attempt to remain competitive. By 1840 the Leeds & Selby line had been extended to Hull and a direct rail link with the Midlands had been opened, thanks to the North Midland Railway line to Derby, where there was an end-on connection with the Derby & Birmingham. At this time, the Leeds & Manchester Railway did not run directly into town but connected with the North Midland at Normanton.

In 1846 the Leeds & Bradford line opened, followed in 1848 by the London & North Western line. In 1849 Headingley and Horsforth were linked by rail to Leeds with the opening of the Leeds Northern to Harrogate. On the eve of the railway amalgamations of 1st January 1923, Leeds was at the centre of a comprehensive railway network and served by five railway companies: the London & North Western, the Midland, the North Eastern, the Lancashire & Yorkshire, and the Great Northern. There were passenger stations at Wellington Street, Leeds Central and Leeds New. Goods facilities were at Wellington Street, Cardigan Road, Hunslet Lane and Central.

Leeds from the Air 1962 AFA99571

The City of Leeds

Many of the pictures in this collection date from around 1900 when Leeds was not only a great engineering centre, but the very hub of the cloth industry. In 1901 the population stood at 428,953 making Leeds the first city in Yorkshire and the fifth in England.

The Town Hall 1894 34765
When Leeds town hall was opened by Queen Victoria, the streets were lined with palm trees and triumphal arches. Designed by Cuthbert Broderick and built between 1853 and 1858, this sumptuous public building was deliberately ambitious in scale, its dignified and spectacular classical lines symbolising Leeds' reputation and position as the leading city of West Riding.

◄ **The Victoria Hall 1888**

20984

The town hall not only housed the council: there were law courts, facilities for lectures, public meetings and for music festivals. This photograph shows the Victoria Hall; the walls are divided into five bays by Corinthian columns, and the stage area is dominated by the organ. The hall was originally called 'the Great Hall', but was dedicated to Queen Victoria after the opening at which she officiated. 200,000 people gathered to watch the ceremony.

The Town Hall, c1965 L28066
When this picture was taken, the town hall, with its 225 ft tower and spectacular frontage of giant columns and pilasters, was in desperate need of a good clean to rid it of decades of soot and grime. In 1972 a proposal for cleaning was at last put on the agenda. However, the Labour group on the council objected, as they did also to the proposed sale of council houses.

The Town Hall and the Headrow c1955
L28004
In 1950 the wool industry was still important to Yorkshire, where 1,123 woollen and worsted mills employed around 150,000. By 1967 there were 825 mills in operation, but by 1986 the figure had dropped to 172.

The War Memorial and the Headrow c1955 L28005
During the First World War, Leeds contributed over 90,000 men to the forces, of whom 9,640 were killed in action. The greatest single loss on one day occurred on 1st July 1916 during the Somme offensive when the Leeds Pals suffered appalling casualties and were all but wiped out.

The Headrow c1965 L28093

This street scene is dominated by the façade of Lewis's store, with its broad plate glass windows and imitation rusticated pillars. It must have appeared very modern when it opened in September 1932. Since then it has changed ownership twice, first becoming part of the Lewis Owen Owen group, and then in 1996 a branch of Allders. The top floor was added at a later date. The dome of the town hall rises over the roofs in the distance.

The City Centre c1965 L28135

The Post Office, with its central turret, was built in 1896 by Sir Henry Tanner. It was erected on the site of the old Mixed Cloth Hall, which was opened in 1756. By the early 18th century, enclosed Cloth Halls in other parts of the county were stealing business from Leeds. A hall for white cloths was opened in Kirkgate in 1711, then replaced by a larger one in 1755.

The City Square and the Queen's Hotel c1965 L28085

At the beginning of the 20th century a room at the Queen's Hotel cost 4s a night, breakfast 3s and dinner 5s. The Great Northern and the Metropole hotels were similarly priced, but the Grand Central in Briggate offered rooms from 4s 6d and dinner at 3s 6d.

The City Square c1965 L28130

On the right is the entrance to Leeds City station. At one time there were three railway stations in the city centre: Central, Wellington and New. In the late 1930s Wellington and New stations were combined and eventually rebuilt as Leeds City, while Central closed in 1967.

The Post Office and Revenue Office 1897
39088
The running of the postal service in Victorian times was considered vital to the public good. The grand and impressive frontage of the Leeds building reflected the Victorians' preoccupation with good communications in their efforts to encourage a prosperous commercial and business community. Post offices had long opening hours. Delivery boys gather outside the main doors, carrying parcels to and from the city's shops and businesses.

The Black Prince Statue c1955 L28015
This statue by Brock is of Edward of Woodstock, better known as the Black Prince on account of his black armour. The son of Edward III, he was already a seasoned warrior at the age of 16, and made his name at Crecy in 1346. He commanded Edward's forces at Poitiers in 1356, a battle in which the French king was captured.

Boar Lane c1965 L28148

Under the Griffin Hotel signboard, and in the midst of the dominating chain stores and offices, Jackson's barber's shop still shows a traditional striped pole. On the left in the distance are the offices of the Provincial Insurance Company and closing the end of the street is the Majestic, where the people of Leeds could enjoy dancing. A Morris Minor heads along Boar Lane towards the City Square. Introduced in 1948 the Minor has since become a classic car enjoying a cult following.

Boar Lane c1965 L28146

Boar Lane bissects Briggate and runs along the southern edge of the commercial heart of the city between Kirkgate and Park Row. Just a few minutes walk from here, the Leeds & Liverpool Canal links up with the River Aire and the Aire & Calder Navigation, providing Leeds with an inland waterway from the Mersey to the Humber.

Schweppes
TABLE WATERS
LONDON & MANCHESTER ASSURANCE Co. LTD
WALKER & HALL SHEFFIELD.
SILVERSMITHS & CUTLERS
WALKER & HALL
LIMITED
WALKER & HALL SHEFFIELD
SILVERSMITHS & CUTLERS
REID BROS
REID BROS
REID BROS
DEWSBURY
WAKEFIELD
DONCASTER

Duncan Street c1955

L28011

This view shows the junction of Boar Lane and Briggate, looking towards the Corn Exchange. In the 17th century Leeds held its cloth fairs at the bottom end of Briggate every Tuesday and Saturday. This was the most important fair in the whole of Yorkshire, attracting traders and customers from miles away. The stalls were set up on the old bridge that spanned the Aire.

Boar Lane c1965 L28147

Partially hidden behind C&A is the Georgian edifice of Holy Trinity church, completed in 1727. It was designed by Halfpenny, with a later 1839 tower and square spire by Chantrell. The street elevations show multiple bays with doorways with Gibbs' surrounds.

New Briggate c1955 L28001

At the beginning of the 20th century Leeds had four theatres, including the Grand, which is featured on the right-hand side of the picture. In the week this photograph was taken you could enjoy a performance of the Royal Carl Rosa Opera. The other Leeds theatres were The Royal in Land's Lane, The Queen's in Meadow Road and the Empire Palace in Briggate.

Briggate c1965 L28142

One of the highlights of shopping along Briggate was the glass-roofed arcades, such as the Queen's and the County. In earlier days Briggate was where the merchants and clothiers assembled to buy and sell cloth, the start of business being heralded by the sounding of the market bell. The street had many small inns for the market customers, built on plots in yards behind the street.

Briggate c1955 L28010
Trams rattle along Briggate in this picture. Leeds was one of the pioneers of segregated tracks, keeping trams and other vehicles apart. The routes to Roundhay, Belle Isle, Middleton, Temple Newsom and Lawnswood were mainly segregated systems and, as a consequence, extremely efficient.

HAM

Briggate c1955 L28012
On the left is Leeds' oldest shop, which dates from 1613 and is receiving a face lift. Further along the street on the right stands the Empire Theatre. There is little architecture remaining of any significance, and the street reveals a complex picture of turreted and pedimented Victorian buildings in a wide range of styles.

The Civic Hall, Calverley Street c1965 L28065

The civic hall was designed by E Vincent Harris and opened with much ceremony in 1933, with temporary stands being erected for spectators. It is curious in that the façade incorporates features in two distinct traditions - the classical four-column portico and pediment, and the Wren-style slim towers. The side elevations, however, are in a more modern style. Behind and to the left are buildings of the Central Colleges.

◄ **Briggate c1965** L28089
Still the principle street for shopping, Briggate's retail outlets included Henry's, Fosters, Paige & Co, and Boots. Also along here were Willerbys and G M Brown's, formerly Lawrence's International Furnishers.

▼ **The Parish Church 1891** 28281
There are no medieval churches in Leeds. The church of St John the Evangelist was consecrated in 1634 and retains its oaken interior and a great screen which is considered to be one of the finest of its type in England. St Peter's in Kirkgate was noted for its 15th-century brasses, whilst 18th-century Holy Trinity in Boar Lane had perhaps the most attractive-looking spire in the area.

◄ **St John's Church 1897** 39094
The interior is unusual, being in the form of two naves, rather than nave and aisle. The 17th-century box pews were irreparably damaged in the 'restoration' of the 1860s by Norman Shaw, when they were cut down. However, the beautiful old screen, with its elaborate strapwork crowns, was retained. On the left is the two-decker pulpit and tester.

The Grammar School 1888 20993
The earliest mention of the provision of education in Leeds dates from 1552 when William Sheafield, chantry priest of St Catherine, left property to support the upkeep of a schoolmaster. This was the beginning of Leeds Grammar School. The heavy Gothic-style building shown here is by E M Barry, the brother of the headmaster of the period, and was built in 1859.

Cookridge Street c1955 L28008
A view of Leeds Mechanics' Institute. This imposing Italianate building, with its lofty round-arched windows, was built by Cuthbert Brodrick in the late 1860s. It later became the Civic Theatre. In June 1840, Thomas Cook arranged a members' excursion to York by way of the Leeds & Selby and the York & North Midlands Railways. The trip was priced at half the normal fare and included tea at York. There were 570 passengers.

Yorkshire College 1894 34767
This was part of the Victoria University, which was constituted in 1880, the other colleges being at Manchester and Liverpool. The colleges went their separate ways in 1904, each becoming an independent university. There were originally four departments: mathematics and experimental physics, geology and mining, chemistry, and textiles.

Yorkshire College 1894 34768
One of the college's more interesting pupils was Joseph Wright who had begun working at Salt's Mill, Saltaire when he was just seven years old. Joseph studied at Yorkshire College and gained entrance to Heidleburg University. He eventually became Professor of Contemporary Philology at Oxford.

▼ **Leeds University, Cloth Workers' Court c1960** L28112
The university launched an appeal in 1925 for £500,000 to build a new medical school, departmental buildings, library and student union. Lord Brotherton donated his collection of rare books and gave £100,000 in cash. Some of the buildings were finished before the start of the Second World War, but the new central block was not completed until 1951.

▼ **Leeds University, The Engineering Building c1960** L28121
One of the university's architecturally more interesting buildings is the Brotherton Library, paid for by Lord Brotherton and containing over 500,000 volumes, including its benefactor's private collection of rare books.

▲ **Leeds University, The Union, Refectory and Textile Buildings, c1960** L28122
When Victoria University broke up in 1904, Leeds was left by far the poor relation, unable to match the financial input enjoyed by Manchester and Liverpool. In the words of Edward Baines Leeds was 'a slower town and our neighbourhood is quieter'.

Leeds University, The Bar, Union Buildings c1965 L28129

This photo was taken in the days of Watney's draught red barrel and 'a Double Diamond Works Wonders' advertising. The only lager on sale was bottled, usually Lowenbrau.

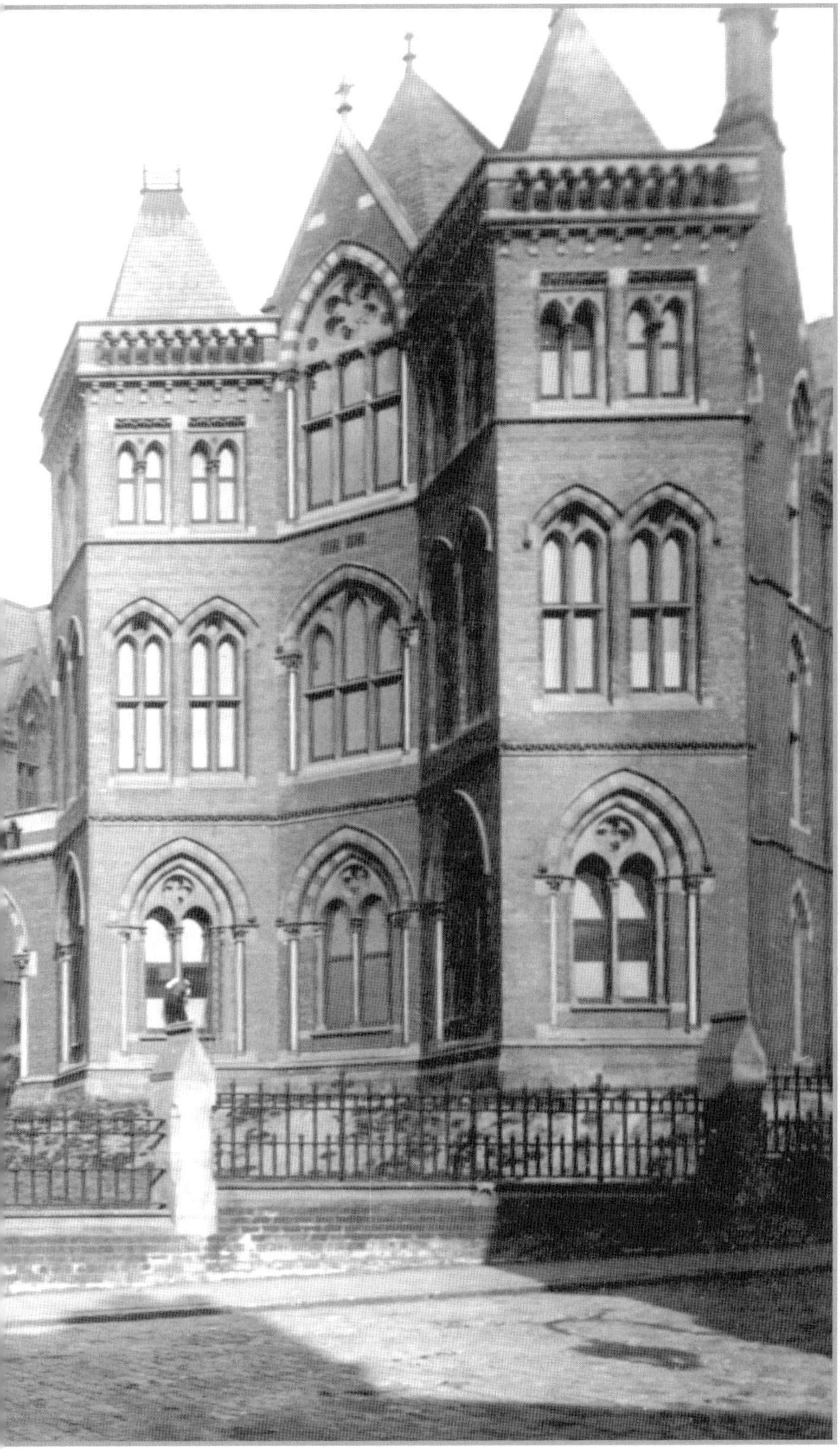

Left: **Leeds Infirmary, Great George Street 1894** 34769
This imposing brick building was built in the Gothic style to the design of George Gilbert Scott in 1868. In the distance is St George's church, another Victorian creation. In March 1809 Mary Bateman, a resident of Leeds, was executed at York. Her body was then taken to the earlier General Infirmary at Leeds where it was exhibited at a charge of 3d a head. Over 2,500 people paid to see her body. Later it was dissected and, following a Yorkshire custom, her skin was tanned and distributed in small pieces to those who applied.

Top left:
The Parkinson Building c1960 L28099
This building, which was part of Leeds University, was designed by T A Lodge and opened in 1951. Its broad tower dominates the city skyline. Frank Parkinson, chairman of Crompton Parkinson and Company, was a student of the Old Yorkshire College in Leeds, and gave a bequest of £200,000 towards the building.

Roundhay Park Lake 1897 39092
Along with Woodhouse Moor to the north, the park was considered the chief lung of the city, where for a few hours at the weekend factory workers had an opportunity to get away from the dust, grime, noise and smell of the workplace.

Roundhay Park 1897 39091
In 1891 the first experiments in England using overhead wiring for electric trams took place on the Roundhay Park route. There were problems caused by the tramway using an earth return for the traction current, and so the line opened using steam tram engines. The electrified route between Kirkstall and Roundhay opened in August 1897.

Roundhay Park 1897 39090
Roundhay Park was purchased by the council in 1872. It comprised 775 acres, including woodlands, lakes and a manor house, part of which was turned into refreshment rooms.

Roundhay Park, The Drinking Fountain c1960 R247005
The council paid £139,000 for the park in 1872, it being one of a number of acquisitions by the authority over the previous 20 years. In 1852, following an outbreak of cholera, the council bought out the private water suppliers for £250,000 and embarked on schemes totalling £4 million, so that by 1918 the city was being supplied with 16 million gallons of fresh water a day. In 1870 the council also acquired control of the Gas Company for £750,000.

Woodhouse Moor 1897 39095
In 1893, a study by a German sociologist found that six out of every seven working-class families in the mill towns of Lancashire and Yorkshire managed to save enough money to spend on a holiday. The money included wages earned by children. In 1841 Thomas Cook organised the earliest-known Sunday excursion with a trip from Leeds to Hull. The train comprised 40 carriages and carried 1,250 passengers.

Woodhouse Moor 1897 39096
This broad space was turned into a public park in 1840. For centuries before it had been a common, where villagers had grazed their cattle. It was embellished by statues of Queen Victoria and Wellington, transferred from Victoria Square. The people of Leeds flocked here at weekends to listen to the band playing and to savour the fresh air.

Temple Newsam Gardens c1960 L28050F
Temple Newsam was bought by Leeds Corporation in 1922 from Edward Wood, the future Lord Halifax. The first house known to have been built here belonged to Thomas, Lord Darcy, who was executed for his involvement in the Yorkshire uprising against the Dissolution. His estate was confiscated by the Crown and later given to Margaret Tudor and her husband the Earl of Lennox. Their son married Mary, Queen of Scots.

W·SMITH
CIGARS
Richmond Gem

Headingley

More than half of Headingley was at one time owned by the Earl of Cardigan, and it was the enclosure of the moor at Far Headingley that had led to its development. After 1821 the village expanded as a result of the opening of several textile factories nearby. Headingley was also an attractive proposition for a growing middle class, able to escape the appalling conditions in Leeds. Those who could afford to were moving to the leafier northern suburbs. Linked to Leeds by rail, horse-drawn omnibus and tram, Headingley's appeal to the middle classes declined after the 1890s, when many workers' houses were built there. However, by 1901 the population stood at 41,561.

Headingley 1894 34773
It would be a few years on before electric street-trams would link Headingley with Leeds city centre. However, in 1894 Leeds corporation took advantage of the Tramways Act of 1870 and bought out the private tramway operators for over £100,000. Horse-drawn trams were replaced on some routes by steam power and electric cars were introduced from 1897.

Headingley, Otley Road c1960 H59026

In this view, taken over sixty years later, the tram lines can still be seen. Headingley had once been a small village to the north of Leeds and its population in 1775 was estimated at 667 people. However, like Leeds the population had doubled by 1801 and continued to rise dramatically over the coming decades.

Headingley, The Parish Church and Old Oak 1897 39097

A view of the spire of St Michael's church, with the remains of the famous Shire Oak, which has a girth of 29 ft. Taylor's Drug Store signboard is almost as big as the shop premises. Boasting branches in London, Leeds, Harrogate and Sunderland, Taylor's claimed they were 'known everywhere' for providing 'the public with pure drugs'.

Headingley, The Parish Church, Nave East 1891 28263
St Michael's church, called 'proud and prosperous' by Pevsner, is by J L Pearson, the architect of Truro Cathedral, and was built in 1885. The high arched ceiling is supported on slim pillars of pale stone, creating a light and welcoming interior. The pulpit is of alabaster and the screen of ironwork. Some critics think the concept a little mechanical in its regularity.

Headingley College 1894 34772

In the latter part of the 19th century, several colleges run by various religious denominations opened around Leeds. The Leeds Clergy school and the Roman Catholic Seminary were both opened in 1876. The Roman Catholic College dates from 1909, whilst the Wesleyan College at Headingley predates them all, being opened in 1868.

Far Headingley, St Chad's Church c1960 F85033

This splendid church was conceived by Sir Edmund Beckett, who as well as being a barrister and amateur architect designed the clock mechanism of Big Ben. St Chad's slender spire soars over the surrounding rooftops and countryside. Chad was a Northumbrian monk appointed bishop of Ite Mercians in 669. He built his cathedral at Lichfield where he died of plague in 672. Chad converted two sons of King Wulfhere of Mercia to Christianity.

Headingley, The Parish Church, Lady Chapel 1891 28264
The chapel was dedicated to the Virgin Mary. In the Lady Chapel of St Edward's at Clifford, there is a statue of the Virgin sculptured by H Hoffman. Hoffman was a Jew who converted to the Catholic faith when carving the image in his studio in Rome.

Headingley, The Cricket Ground Pavilion 1897 39099
Originally a part of the Cardigan Fields estate, Headingley was put on the market in 1888 and purchased by the Leeds cricket and football clubs in January 1889. The first cricket match was played at Headingley in 1890, and Yorkshire County matches transferred to to the ground from the previous county pitch at Sheffield. Test cricket began at Headingley in 1899.

ELECTRICITY
Service Centre
EEDS INDUSTRIAL CO-OPERATIVE SOCIETY LTD.
TELEPHONE
CAR PARK
CINEMA
3550 UB
6620 NW

Horsforth

This town, situated at the north-western edge of Leeds, remained independent until the local government reorganisation of 1974. Along with Pudsey, Yeadon, Aireborough, Otley, Harewood, Bardsey, Linton, Wetherby, Boston Spa, Aberford, Garforth, Ledsham, Rothwell and Morley, it became a part of the City of Leeds Metropolitan District.

Horsforth, Town Street c1960 H118032
No town centre worth its salt was complete without its Co-op store. On the left in this picture is the branch of the Leeds Industrial Co-operative Society. Every customer had a membership number against which all transactions were logged. One of the great occasions in the Co-op year was going to collect the family dividend or 'divi'. The divi was the membership share of what would have been a retailer's profit after all expenses. It varied from one society to another, and could be anything from 1s 6d to 3s in the pound. Beyond the Co-op is the Imperial Cinema. On the extreme left is the Electricity Service Centre. Throughout the 1950s and 60s the standard of living continued to rise, and people invested in household aids such as washing machines, fridges and televisions.

GOOD STABLING
&
BILLIARD ROOM
KINGS ARMS HOTEL.
HORSFORTH HARRIERS

Horsforth, Town Street 1901 47133
A horse takes a breather and feeds from its nosebag on the pavement. The cart on the left looks like a brewer's dray - in the back are barrels - and is probably delivering to the Black Bull on the right. There was probably strong competition between the Black Bull and the Old King's Arms across the street - the latter boasts a billiard room and is the meeting place for the Horsforth Harriers.

◂ **Horsforth, New Road Side c1960** H118049
Cinema in 1960 was still a popular form of entertainment, though television and the opportunities opened up by private car ownership were both beginning to make inroads. In the week this photograph was taken, cinema-goers to the Glenroyal were enjoying 'The Day They Robbed the Bank of England'. The building is now a supermarket.

◄ **Horsforth, The Green c1965** H118106
Instead of horses and carts, cars now clog the pavement outside the Black Bull. Note how the dark ashlar is picked out by severe white mortaring. The broad signboards still squats awkwardly over the first-floor bay windows.

▼ **Horsforth, Shopping in New Road Side c1965**
H118094
This was the period when few supermarkets existed and those that did were built in town centres, as most people relied on public transport. New Road Side is here still a street of small, traditional shops.

◄ **Horsforth, Town Street c1965** H118109
By this time the small shop was under serious threat. Drifut's, on the extreme left, is offering customers coloured sand shoes and baseball boots to augment its traditional old-style repair business. The headquarters of the local Liberal Club would appear to be in the room upstairs.

Horsforth, The Mechanics' Institute 1901 47134
This building is still standing in Town Street, and was built in the early 1880s in local stone quarried at Golden Bank. Stone from the same quarry was used in the construction of the seafront at Scarborough. The Institute has retained its educational function, and now provides community classes of all kinds for the people of Horsforth. Such institutions had spread rapidly during the 19th century and provided workers with an opportunity to undertake education courses backed up with examinations.

Horsforth, The Ring Road Roundabout c1960 H118026

In 1934 Leeds City Council embarked on a programme to clear 30,000 slums. Delayed by the outbreak of the Second World War, the programme continued in the 1940s and included plans to build 53,000 new homes. However, building always lagged behind demand. Great swathes of countryside were cut through to make roads and roundabouts.

Horsforth, Springfield Hospital 1901 47149

This modest hospital was set up in Scotland Lane as the Leeds Work People's Convalescent Home. Members would pay their 1d a week and be entitled to rest and recuperation here. It later fell derelict and became in succession, a home for sufferers from Cerebral Palsy and for Bosnian refugees.

Horsforth, Woodside Church 1901 47144
Among the more colourful sects to establish themselves in Leeds were the Swedenborgians and the Inghamites. The Swedenborgians arrived in 1816 but struggled to survive, and were without a minister for almost 50 years. The Inghamites, once a force to be reckoned with in the Leeds area, declined throughout the 1870s and 80s, and finally disbanded in the 1890s.

Horsforth, Woodside Wesleyan Chapel 1901 47145
In Outwood Lane, this building is now the Woodside Methodist Church. Between 1840 and 1885 only one new Wesleyan chapel was opened in Leeds: at Roscoe Place in 1861. Wesleyan membership declined within Leeds during the 1840s and 50s but seems to have held up in the surrounding townships, such as Horsforth. New missions to these places led to a spate of chapel building in the late 19th century.

Horsforth, The Grove Wesleyan Church 1901 47138
This is not the original Wesleyan church in Horsforth - it replaced a building of 1786. It is an unusual structure, with a double-doored porch, and was built in 1868. The date stone states 1867, but completion was delayed by snow. The Wesleyans were the first to open a college in the Leeds area: at Headingley in 1868. In 1816 they had opened the first night school, where young men aged 15 and over could attend and learn to read and write.

Horsforth, Newlay Wood 1901 47147
Within the Leeds city boundary most of the open areas between the townships gradually dispersed under an urban sprawl of industrial and housing development. Horsforth survived as an independent borough until 1974, when it was swallowed up in the City of Leeds Metropolitan District.

Horsforth, The Hall 1901 47139
This lovely old hall was requisitioned by the local council around the time of the Second World War. However, they failed to bring it the care and attention it deserved and dry rot soon set in. At one point the Clerk of the Council's chair disappeared through the floor! It was demolished in the early 1950s.

Horsforth, Hall Park 1901 47140
This picturesque park was presented to the townspeople by William Mathieson of Wilson and Mathieson of Armley.

Kirkstall Abbey

Henry de Lacy, Lord of Pontefract, was seriously ill and was expected to die. If he survived, Henry promised to build a monastery in honour of the Blessed Virgin. In fact, he did survive and Henry kept his promise, giving the abbot of Fountains Abbey land to build on at Barnoldswick. The abbot for the new Cistercian House came from Skeildale, near Ripon; however, the new site did not prove suitable, and Abbot Alexander decided that he and his brethren should move somewhere else. The site they chose was Kirkstall.

Kirkstall like other Cistercian Houses grew rich on wool, and the abbey is thought to have been awarded the charter to hold Wibsey Fair, one of the oldest in England. In order to finance their ever-grander building projects, the Cistercians were quite willing to sell wool for several years ahead by means of advanced contracts. Sometimes, building costs and income did not balance. In 1275 Fountains Abbey had to be bailed out of its financial difficulties by the Jews of York. The abbey was in the red to the tune of £6,000, a phenomenal amount of money in those days.

Kirkstall Abbey, From the Weir 1891 28284
After the Dissolution, the abbey was left a ruin and many of its stones were eventually carted off and used to widen the old Leeds Bridge. Even so the chapter house, cloisters and abbot's lodging are still impressive.

Kirkstall Abbey 1891 28285

The abbey played a part in the industrial development of Leeds, for it was here that iron forging first began in the district. Kirkstall was founded in 1152 as a daughter house of Fountains Abbey. Building work was completed by 1175 and iron forging began in 1200.

Kirkstall Abbey, The Western Facade c1861 7411

Kirkstall is one of the finest and most complete examples of early Cistercian architecture in Britain. The main entrance to the abbey church was through this imposing porch, enriched with capitals with scalloped details. The original circular window above was replaced by the two round-arched windows in the late 15th century.

Kirkstall Abbey, The Nave c1955 K40003F

This view shows the prospect as revealed through the west door, seen in the previous photograph. This long and lofty space was originally divided into smaller chapels and areas where lay brothers could worship. At the back of the great columns were screens closing off the side aisles. A stone screen or pulpitum straddled the nave, surounded by a gallery from which the gospel was sung on festival days. Beyond the tower crossing was the choir, where the monks sat and chanted in wooden stalls.

Kirkstall Abbey 1891 28289

Cleanliness in the 12th and 13th centuries was certainly next to Godliness. The Cistercians, like the Knights Templar, were not noted for their standards of personal hygiene and rarely washed. At Kirkstall the monks had the benefit of piped water so that they might wet rather than wash their hands before entering the refectory. There was also a bath, but its use was probably limited. The Catholic Church considered bathing in public to be sinful, though taking the waters at holy wells to relieve aches and pains was acceptable.

Kirkstall, St Stephen's Church 1894 34775

This curious building, with tall, slim lancets extending almost from floor to roof, was conceived by R D Chantrell in 1828; Chantrell was responsible for a number of Gothic-revival inspired churches in the Leeds region.
St Stephen's has a west tower with a spire and was almost entirely altered internally in the late Victorian period.

Continental
Motor-Tyres

Wetherby

Set at the extreme north-eastern edge of the City of Leeds Metropolitan District, Wetherby was once an important stop-over and relay station for stagecoaches travelling the Great North Road. With the coming of the railways, long-distance stagecoach travel quickly became outmoded. Wetherby went into decline, relying on tourist traffic instead of scheduled coaches.

Left: **Wetherby, North Street 1909** 61731
Ward & Sons was established in 1868 and had probably been smiths and farriers until they resolved to concentrate on repairing vehicles and selling bicycles. As can be seen from the picture, they were also the local agent for the AA. Further down the street, Continental Motors is the local agent for Michelin.

Below: **Wetherby, Market Place 1909** 61729
At the turn of the century Wetherby was described in some tourist guides as 'a town of no interest'. In 1920 all the influential Dunlop Guide could find to say about the town was that it had 'pleasant walks by the river'. Wetherby was famed for its ancient Thursday market and fair, sanctioned by the Knights Templar. The town hall was built in 1845.

MOTORISTS CATERED FOR
THE ANGEL HOTEL
HORSE FAIR
PHONE 0200.
SONS
SHELL

Wetherby,
High Street 1909
61730
The Angel Hotel was one of three hotels that catered for motorists, the others being the George and Dragon, and the Brunswick. The Angel was a substantial establishment, with stabling for a hundred horses. Forty pairs of horses were maintained at the inn for posting.

CHAPPELL
CHYMIST & DRUGGIST

Boston Spa
& the Yorkshire Woollen District

In 1744 a man named John Shires discovered a saline spring at Boston. Taking the waters was a popular and fashionable pastime of the period, and it was not long before Boston developed into a popular spa. However, the town's moment of glory was brief: like several other minor Yorkshire spas it could not hope to compete with the likes of Harrogate and Scarborough, and lacked the social life of Ilkley and Malton.

The Yorkshire Woollen District included within its boundaries Wakefield, Osset, Castleford, Normanton, Pontefract, Dewsbury, Batley, Birstall, Heckmondwicke and Morley. Though the woollen industry dominated the

(continued overleaf)

Boston Spa, High Street 1893 32000
This view reveals Boston's elegant and urbane character. Handsome and dignified Georgian houses and villas line the leafy street. Visitors to the town seem to have been made up from two groups: travellers using the Great North Road, who stopped over just long enough to sample the waters in the Pump Room before departing for more sophisticated destinations; and the citizens of Leeds who made the place popular enough for a daily stagecoach service to operate.

area, there was also a substantial coalmining presence, especially around the towns of Castleford and Pontefract. There were other industries too, including chemicals, engineering and glassmaking.

The geography of the district, which measures approximately 22 miles wide by nine or ten miles deep, differs between east and west. The western area is noted for its deep valleys along which the mill towns were established. The eastern area is much flatter and is where the majority of coalmining took place.

Morley, Queens Street c1965 M149014

Looming over the town is the tower of the town hall, clearly more than a little influenced in its design by its more prestigious neighbour at Leeds. It was built in 1895 by G A Fox, with a portico formed of six composite columns. Until recent times textile mills jostled the building. As a part of the Heavy Woollen District of Dewsbury and the Spen Valley, Morley suffered during the slump of the 1930s. Bewteen 1924 and 1930 over 46,000 jobs were lost in the woollen industry, most of them in Yorkshire.

Morley, Queens Street c1965 M149009
After the 1930s the next blow to the Woollen District came in the 1960s with the import of cheap Italian heavy-woollen skirtings and coatings. Even after taking transportation costs into account, cheap labour enabled the Italians to undersell heavy-woollen Yorkshire-made products.

Morley, The Grammar School c1965 M149016
Severely modern and uncompromising in its architecture, this grammar school symbolised the progressive educational changes of the post-war period. In 1966 proposals were put forward to reorganise the education system within 15 years. It was decreed that all children aged 11 to 18 years would attend comprehensive schools. In the interim period comprehensives were split between those taking 11 to 13 year olds, and those taking 13 to 18 year olds.

Brick Works
Div. of Parly. Boro. Bdy.
CEMETERY
Chapel
WOODHOUSE
Reservoir
Malthouse
Hill Top
Ch.
Grammar School
COLLEGE
Chapel
Vicarage
School
Schools
Chap.
R.C. Seminary
Sch.
Iron Works
Denison Hall
HANOVER SQUARE
Club
Church
INFIRMARY
Mill
Dye Works
Albion Works
Iron Works
WEST ST.
PARK SQUARE
Church
Ch.
WELLINGTON STREET
Wellington Br.
Mills
Sta.
Chapel
Gas Works
Engine Sheds
Mills
Monk Br.
Sta.
Schs.

ORDNANCE SURVEY MAP OF LEEDS *1890*

Index

The Francis Frith Collection Titles

www.francisfrith.com

The Francis Frith Collection publishes over 100 new titles each year. A selection of those currently available is listed below. For latest catalogue please contact The Francis Frith Collection. ***Town Books*** 96 pages, approximately 75 photos. ***County and Themed Books*** 128 pages, approximately 135 photos (unless specified). All titles hardback with laminated case and jacket, except those indicated pb (paperback)

Accrington Old and New
Alderley Edge and Wilmslow
Amersham, Chesham and Rickmansworth
Andover
Around Abergavenny
Around Alton
Aylesbury
Barnstaple
Bedford
Bedfordshire
Berkshire Living Memories
Berkshire PA
Blackpool Pocket Album
Bognor Regis
Bournemouth
Bradford
Bridgend
Bridport
Brighton and Hove
Bristol
Buckinghamshire
Calne Living Memories
Camberley PA
Canterbury Cathedral
Cardiff Old and New
Chatham and the Medway Towns
Chelmsford
Chepstow Then and Now
Cheshire
Cheshire Living Memories
Chester
Chesterfield
Chigwell
Christchurch
Churches of East Cornwall
Clevedon
Clitheroe
Corby Living Memories
Cornish Coast
Cornwall Living Memories
Cotswold Living Memories
Cotswold Pocket Album
Coulsdon, Chipstead and Woodmanstern
County Durham
Cromer, Sheringham and Holt
Dartmoor Pocket Album
Derby
Derbyshire
Derbyshire Living Memories
Devon
Devon Churches
Dorchester
Dorset Coast PA
Dorset Living Memories
Dorset Villages
Down the Dart
Down the Severn
Down the Thames
Dunmow, Thaxted and Finchingfield
Durham
East Anglia PA
East Devon
East Grinstead
Edinburgh
Ely and The Fens
Essex PA
Essex Second Selection
Essex: The London Boroughs
Exeter
Exmoor
Falmouth
Farnborough, Fleet and Aldershot
Folkestone
Frome
Furness and Cartmel Peninsulas
Glamorgan
Glasgow
Glastonbury
Gloucester
Gloucestershire
Greater Manchester
Guildford
Hailsham
Hampshire
Harrogate
Hastings and Bexhill
Haywards Heath Living Memories
Heads of the Valleys
Heart of Lancashire PA
Helston
Herefordshire
Horsham
Humberside PA
Huntingdon, St Neots and St Ives
Hythe, Romney Marsh and Ashford
Ilfracombe
Ipswich PA
Isle of Wight
Isle of Wight Living Memories
King's Lynn
Kingston upon Thames
Lake District PA
Lancashire Living Memories
Lancashire Villages

Available from your local bookshop or from the publisher

The Francis Frith Collection Titles (continued)

Lancaster, Morecombe and Heysham Pocket Album
Leeds PA
Leicester
Leicestershire
Lincolnshire Living Memoires
Lincolnshire Pocket Album
Liverpool and Merseyside
London PA
Ludlow
Maidenhead
Maidstone
Malmesbury
Manchester PA
Marlborough
Matlock
Merseyside Living Memories
Nantwich and Crewe
New Forest
Newbury Living Memories
Newquay to St Ives
North Devon Living Memories
North London
North Wales
North Yorkshire
Northamptonshire
Northumberland
Northwich
Nottingham
Nottinghamshire PA
Oakham
Odiham Then and Now
Oxford Pocket Album
Oxfordshire
Padstow
Pembrokeshire
Penzance
Petersfield Then and Now
Plymouth
Poole and Sandbanks
Preston PA
Ramsgate Old and New
Reading Pocket Album
Redditch Living Memories
Redhill to Reigate
Rhondda Valley Living Mems
Richmond
Ringwood
Rochdale
Romford PA
Salisbury PA
Scotland
Scottish Castles
Sevenoaks and Tonbridge
Sheffield and South Yorkshire PA
Shropshire
Somerset
South Devon Coast
South Devon Living Memories
South East London
Southampton PA
Southend PA
Southport
Southwold to Aldeburgh
Stourbridge Living Memories
Stratford upon Avon
Stroud
Suffolk
Suffolk PA
Surrey Living Memories
Sussex
Sutton
Swanage and Purbeck
Swansea Pocket Album
Swindon Living Memories
Taunton
Teignmouth
Tenby and Saundersfoot
Tiverton
Torbay
Truro
Uppingham
Villages of Kent
Villages of Surrey
Villages of Sussex PA
Wakefield and the Five Towns Living Memories
Warrington
Warwick
Warwickshire PA
Wellingborough Living Memories
Wells
Welsh Castles
West Midlands PA
West Wiltshire Towns
West Yorkshire
Weston-super-Mare
Weymouth
Widnes and Runcorn
Wiltshire Churches
Wiltshire Living memories
Wiltshire PA
Wimborne
Winchester PA
Windermere
Windsor
Wirral
Wokingham and Bracknell
Woodbridge
Worcester
Worcestershire
Worcestershire Living Memories
Wyre Forest
York PA
Yorkshire
Yorkshire Coastal Memories
Yorkshire Dales
Yorkshire Revisited

FRITH PRODUCTS & SERVICES

Francis Frith would doubtless be pleased to know that the pioneering publishing venture he started in 1860 still continues today. Over a hundred and forty years later, The Francis Frith Collection continues in the same innovative tradition and is now one of the foremost publishers of vintage photographs in the world. Some of the current activities include:

Interior Decoration

Today Frith's photographs can be seen framed and as giant wall murals in thousands of pubs, restaurants, hotels, banks, retail stores and other public buildings throughout the country. In every case they enhance the unique local atmosphere of the places they depict and provide reminders of gentler days in an increasingly busy and frenetic world.

Product Promotions

Frith products are used by many major companies to promote the sales of their own products or to reinforce their own history and heritage. Frith promotions have been used by Hovis bread, Courage beers, Scots Porage Oats, Colman's mustard, Cadbury's foods, Mellow Birds coffee, Dunhill pipe tobacco, Guinness, and Bulmer's Cider.

Genealogy and Family History

As the interest in family history and roots grows world-wide, more and more people are turning to Frith's photographs of Great Britain for images of the towns, villages and streets where their ancestors lived; and, of course, photographs of the churches and chapels where their ancestors were christened, married and buried are an essential part of every genealogy tree and family album.

Frith Products

All Frith photographs are available Framed or just as Mounted Prints and Posters (size 23 x 16 inches). These may be ordered from the address below. From time to time other products - Address Books, Calendars, Table Mats, etc - are available.

The Internet

Already ninety thousand Frith photographs can be viewed and purchased on the internet through the Frith websites and a myriad of partner sites.

For more detailed information on Frith companies and products, look at this sites:

www.francisfrith.com

See the complete list of Frith Books at:

www.francisfrith.com

This web site is regularly updated with the latest list of publications from The Francis Frith Collection. If you wish to buy books relating to another part of the country that your local bookshop does not stock, you may purchase on-line.

For further information, trade, or author enquiries please contact us at the address below:

The Francis Frith Collection, Frith's Barn, Teffont, Salisbury, Wiltshire, England SP3 5QP.

Tel: +44 (0)1722 716 376 Fax: +44 (0)1722 716 881 Email: sales@francisfrith.co.uk

See Frith books on the internet at www.francisfrith.com

FREE PRINT OF YOUR CHOICE

Mounted Print
Overall size 14 x 11 inches (355 x 280mm)

Choose any Frith photograph in this book. Simply complete the Voucher opposite and return it with your remittance for £3.50 (to cover postage and handling) and we will print the photograph of your choice in SEPIA (size 11 x 8 inches) and supply it in a cream mount with a burgundy rule line (overall size 14 x 11 inches). **Please note: aerial photographs and photographs with a reference number starting with a "Z" are not Frith photographs and cannot be supplied under this offer. Offer valid for delivery to one UK address only.**

***PLUS:* Order additional Mounted Prints at HALF PRICE - £9.50 each** (normally £19.00)
If you would like to order more Frith prints from this book, possibly as gifts for friends and family, you can buy them at half price (with no additional postage and handling costs).

***PLUS:* Have your Mounted Prints framed**
For an extra £18.00 per print you can have your mounted print(s) framed in an elegant polished wood and gilt moulding, overall size 16 x 13 inches (no additional postage and handling required).

IMPORTANT!

These special prices are only available if you use this form to order. You must use the ORIGINAL VOUCHER on this page (no copies permitted). We can only despatch to one UK address. This offer cannot be combined with any other offer.

Send completed Voucher form to:
The Francis Frith Collection, Frith's Barn, Teffont, Salisbury, Wiltshire SP3 5QP

CHOOSE A PHOTOGRAPH FROM THIS BOOK

Voucher *for **FREE** and Reduced Price Frith Prints*

Please do not photocopy this voucher. Only the original is valid, so please fill it in, cut it out and return it to us with your order.

Picture ref no	Page no	Qty	Mounted @ £9.50	Framed + £18.00	Total Cost £
		1	Free of charge*	£	£
			£9.50	£	£
			£9.50	£	£
			£9.50	£	£
			£9.50	£	£
			£9.50	£	£
			* Post & handling		£3.50
			Total Order Cost		£

Please allow 28 days for delivery. Offer available to one UK address only

Title of this book . . . .
I enclose a cheque/postal order for £ . . . .
made payable to 'The Francis Frith Collection'

OR please debit my Mastercard / Visa / Maestro card, details below

Card Number

Issue No (Maestro only) Valid from (Maestro)

Expires Signature

Name Mr/Mrs/Ms ....
Address ....
....
....
.... Postcode ....
Daytime Tel No ....
Email ....

978-1-85937-202-3 Valid to 31/12/12

Free Print - see overleaf

Can you help us with information about any of the Frith photographs in this book?

We are gradually compiling an historical record for each of the photographs in the Frith archive. It is always fascinating to find out the names of the people shown in the pictures, as well as insights into the shops, buildings and other features depicted.

If you recognize anyone in the photographs in this book, or if you have information not already included in the author's caption, do let us know. We would love to hear from you, and will try to publish it in future books or articles.

Our production team

Frith books are produced by a small dedicated team at offices in the converted Grade II listed 18th-century barn at Teffont near Salisbury, illustrated above. Most have worked with The Francis Frith Collection for many years. All have in common one quality: they have a passion for The Francis Frith Collection. The team is constantly expanding, but currently includes:

Andrew Alsop, Paul Baron, Jason Buck, John Buck, Jenny Coles, Heather Crisp, David Davies, Natalie Davis, Louis du Mont, Isobel Hall, Chris Hardwick, Julian Hight, Peter Horne, James Kinnear, Karen Kinnear, Tina Leary, Stuart Login, Sue Molloy, Sarah Roberts, Kate Rotondetto, Eliza Sackett, Terence Sackett, Sandra Sampson, Adrian Sanders, Sandra Sanger, Julia Skinner, Lewis Taylor, Will Tunnicliffe, David Turner and Ricky Williams.